Reykjavik Pocket Tr

"Explore Reykjavik with the comprehensive Pocket Guidebook. Explore enchanting Northern Lights viewing spots, embark on a self-guided Reykjavik tour, and uncover hidden gems across the breathtaking Icelandic landscape. Packed with insider tips, it's your ultimate companion for an immersive and unforgettable journey through the Land of Fire and Ice."

William's B. Braden

All rights reserved. No part of this publication may be reproduced, distributed, or transmitted in any form or by any means, including photocopying, recording, or other electronic or mechanical methods, without the prior written permission of the publisher, except in the case of brief quotations embodied in critical reviews and certain other noncommercial uses permitted by copyright law.

Copyright ©William's B. Braden,2023

Table of Content

Introduction
About The Author

Chapter 1
History and cultural
Hallgrimskirkja
Harpa
National museum of Iceland
The old harbor
Reykjavik art museum
Reykjavik, maritime museum
Perlan
Arbaejarsafn open air museum
Blue lagoon
Golden cycle.

Chapter 2
~Visa and entry requirements in Reykjavik
~Things to pack on your travel preparation to Reykjavik, Iceland:

Chapter 3
To places To Visit.

Hallgrimskirkja and around
Laugavegur the main shopping streets
Safnahúsiò and Harpa
Austurvöllur and Aðalstræti
Tjörnin and around
Graidi
Eastwards to Laugardalur
Perlan, öskjuhlið and nauthólsvík
Seltjarnarnes
Greater Reykjavik.

Chapter 4
Transport options.
Best Dining and entertainment restaurants in Reykjavik, Iceland.

Chapter 5
Accommodations options in Reykjavik, Iceland:
Homestay
Hotels and
Rentals

Chapter 6
Best time to Visit
Children attraction and activities
Outdoors Activities

Chapter 7
14 days itinerary in Reykjavik, Iceland

Chapter 8
Best time to visit Reykjavik.
Tips and Essential information needed for Travelers Visiting Reykjavik, Iceland.

Chapter 9
Reykjavik, Iceland cultural experience and Festivals
Souvenir Shopping in Reykjavik, Iceland.

Introduction

About The Author.

When William's B. Braden happened upon a worn-out Reykjavik trip guide at a nearby bookstore, his curiosity was piqued. Curious, he dreamed of seeing the wonders of Iceland. He left for Reykjavik with his luggage packed a year later, fascinated by the region of fire and ice.

William enjoyed the local specialties, discovered hidden jewels, and fully immersed himself in the lively culture. He discovered that previous guidebooks overlooked subtle personal aspects that are essential for a genuine experience as his Icelandic trip developed. Motivated, he made the decision to produce his own—EXPLORE Reykjavik Travel Planning Guide.

William created a book that reflected his experiences, from the breathtaking Northern Lights to little neighborhood eateries, by drawing on anecdotes from real life. His handbook captured the spirit of Iceland, providing useful advice, cultural insights, and unconventional suggestions. Written with passion, it reflected his voyage into the centre of Reykjavik, away from the mainstream.

News of William's unique guidebook—celebrated for its authenticity—began to circulate. EXPLORE Reykjavik was the goal of tourists who wanted to see the city through William's eyes. His creation encouraged others to go beyond the norm and is proof of a journey that went beyond tourism.

Once a keen traveler, William's B. Braden unintentionally bridged the gap between official travel guides and real encounters. In order to ensure that every traveler might experience Iceland's charm as deeply as he had, EXPLORE Reykjavik evolved into more than just a book. It became a story, a friend, and a window into Reykjavik's spirit.

History and cultural Reykjavik, Iceland

The origins of Reykjavik may be traced to Norse settlers who settled on the coasts of what is now Reykjavik in the ninth century under the leadership of Ingólfur Arnarson. The name of the city, which means "Smoky Bay," is thought to have sprung from the geothermal steam that rose from the nearby hot springs.

The relationship between Þingvellir and Parliament:

At Þingvellir, on the Golden Circle, the first national parliament of Iceland, Alþingi, was established in 930 AD. One of the world's oldest assemblies, it was essential to Iceland's governmental structure and legal framework. Þingvellir National Park is now recognised as a World Heritage Site by UNESCO.

Cultural and Literary Heritage: The sagas, or medieval literary works that document the history and folklore of Iceland, are a fundamental part of Icelandic culture. A key work of Icelandic literature is Snorri Sturluson's 13th-century Snorra Edda. Founded in 1908, the Reykjavik City Library still promotes a passion for reading and learning.

The Lutheran Cathedral and Harpa Concert Hall: Hallgrímskirkja, a Lutheran church that represents contemporary Icelandic architecture, adorns Reykjavik's skyline. Guðjón Samúelsson designed one of the tallest buildings in the nation. Harpa Concert Hall is a center for cultural events and performances and has a spectacular glass exterior that embodies modern design.

Independence and the Modern Era: On June 17, 1944—the National Day of Iceland—Iceland declared its independence from Denmark. The nation developed into a cutting-edge, progressive nation renowned for its dedication to environmental sustainability, renewable energy, and gender equality.

Art and Museums: The National Gallery of Iceland, one of Iceland's premier art institutions, features both modern and 19th-century Icelandic art, contributing to the city's thriving art culture. The Reykjavik Art Museum honors both domestic and foreign artists and is housed at several locations. A singular example of Iceland's diverse museum scene is the Phallological Museum.

Annual Events: Reykjavik is home to a number of colorful cultural events, such as the Reykjavik International Film Festival and the Reykjavik Arts Festival. Iceland Airwaves is a music event that draws performers from all over the world, adding to the vibrant cultural environment of the city.

Modern Reykjavik: Reykjavik in the modern era is a hive of inventiveness, inclusivity, and originality. The city's buildings are covered in street art, which reflects a spirit of uniqueness and expression. The Reykjavik City Museum, galleries, and cafés are some of the cultural venues that add to the city's international atmosphere.

In conclusion, Reykjavik has developed into a vibrant center of culture despite its roots in Viking colonization and parliamentary government.

Reykjavik embraces the spirit of current inventiveness and diversity while celebrating its legacy through events ranging from literary sagas to festivals of modern art.

Chapter 1

Exploring Reykjavik

Hallgrimskirkja

Reykjavik, Iceland's most famous feature is the lofty Hallgrímskirkja, the nation's largest church. Completed in 1986, the building's distinctive style, with a concrete facade modelled after volcanic basalt columns, is symbolic of the nation's natural surroundings. It was designed by architect Guðjón Samúelsson.

The church is named after the clergyman and poet Hallgrímur Pétursson of Iceland, and the play of light and shadow, as well as the country's basalt rocks, are thought to have inspired the design. Reykjavik can be seen from Hallgrímskirkja's tower, which gives sweeping views of the city and its environs.

Explore the church's interior, which has a tasteful yet understated style. The enormous pipe organ, created by German organ builder Johannes Klais, is the focal point. The church frequently holds concerts, enhancing its cultural relevance with a musical component.

A must-see for anybody visiting Reykjavik, Hallgrímskirkja is a place of worship as well as a representation of Iceland's rich cultural legacy and stunning surroundings.

~Harpa

Welcome to Harpa, the cultural center and architectural wonder of Reykjavik. If you've never been here before, get ready to be enthralled by this magnificent performance venue and convention centre that stands majestically along the city's waterfront.

Architectural Marvel: Harpa is a modern architectural marvel, with its unique façade created by famous artist Olafur Eliasson in partnership with Henning Larsen Architects. It mimics the movement of light and sea and is made up of geometric glass panels that imitate Iceland's natural landscapes. The building has a crystalline appearance.

Concerts and Events: Harpa is a thriving centre of culture, not only a sight to behold. For a variety of performances, seminars, and concerts, check out the event calendar. Events held in the major concert hall, Eldborg Hall, range from festivals of contemporary music to classical symphonies. To ensure a fully immersive experience, make sure to purchase tickets in advance.

Guided Tours: If you want to learn more about the history and architecture of Harpa, think about going on a guided tour. Skilled tour leaders offer valuable perspectives on the architecture, cultural relevance, and construction history of the building. Visits to the intriguing organ, backstage spaces, and principal halls are usually included on tours.

Harpa's Organ: It's imperative to view the Klais organ, a masterpiece within a masterpiece. Made by the well-known German organ builder Johannes Klais, it has more than 5,000 pipes and is a musical marvel. Devoting yourself to the complexities of this instrument is a rewarding experience, even in the absence of a concert.

Dining with a View: Reykjavik and the surrounding mountains may be seen from a number of the dining options available at Harpa. The on-site restaurants serve a variety of cuisines, whether you're in the mood for foreign or Icelandic specialties. For a special meal, think about reserving a table with a view.

Shopping & Souvenirs: Take a look around Harpa's gift shops before you depart. You may purchase one-of-a-kind souvenirs to remember your visit, ranging from modern designs to traditional Icelandic crafts.

Availability:

Harpa is conveniently close to Reykjavik's downtown, making it simple to get to on foot or by public transportation. There are lots of places in the neighbourhood to take a leisurely stroll along the waterfront.

In summary, Harpa is a cultural treasure trove that skillfully combines innovative architecture with a diverse range of activities and events. Whether you're a lover of music, an expert in architecture, or just an inquisitive tourist, Harpa guarantees an unforgettable trip into the center of Iceland's creative and cultural scene.

National Museum of Iceland.

The National Museum of Iceland, tucked away in the centre of Reykjavik, provides an engrossing voyage through the rich history, culture, and legacy of the nation. Here's all the information you need to know as a first-time guest to ensure a fulfilling encounter.

Architectural Marvel: An holistic investigation of Iceland's past is made possible by the museum's architecture, which combines traditional and modern aspects. The structure itself is an artistic creation that welcomes guests with open arms.

Collections and displays: The museum's carefully chosen displays take visitors on a tour of Iceland's history, from the country's colonisation to the present. Admire mediaeval manuscripts and Viking relics while discovering the cultural development of the country. The Íslendingur, a Viking ship replica that went to North America, and the Silver Treasure, which features fine mediaeval silver items, are noteworthy attractions.

Interactive exhibits: Take part in exhibits that make history come to life. The museum provides creative means of establishing a connection with Iceland's past, whether through multimedia displays or virtual reality experiences. It's an informative and enjoyable visit thanks to these interactive features that cater to visitors of all ages.

Guided Tours: Take into consideration going on a guided tour to gain a deeper grasp of the historical background and exhibitions. Intriguing tales and insights are shared by knowledgeable guides, who also address any queries you might have. It's a great way to make the most of your time at the museum.

Temporary Exhibitions: Look for shows that focus on certain facets of Icelandic history, art, or culture on the museum's agenda. Every visit may bring something fresh and fascinating thanks to these revolving exhibits.

Museum Store: Look through the museum store before you go to find interesting mementos. Books about Icelandic sagas and handcrafted handicrafts from the area are among the many treasures found at the shop, which showcases the nation's cultural character.

Facilities for Guests:

Essential facilities are available for visitors to the National Museum of Iceland, such as a café where you may unwind and consider your time spent at the museum. You may instantly share your discoveries with friends and family thanks to the free Wi-Fi that is provided.

Location and Easily Achievable:

The museum is ideally located in the heart of Reykjavik and is easily reachable on foot or by public transportation. Think about extending your stay to see the city's lovely streets and neighbouring attractions.

Overview, Iceland's National Museum serves as a portal to the fascinating history of the country. Regardless matter your interest in history or just

general curiosity, this museum provides an in-depth
and captivating look into Iceland's cultural past.

The old harbor

Visit Reykjavik's Old Harbour, a charming jewel with a rich maritime past, to experience its allure and lively ambience. Here is a guide to help you get the most out of your visit to this historic waterfront region.

Historic Maritime Heritage: The heart of Reykjavik's maritime past is located in the Old Harbour. Take a stroll along the docks where antique ships and fishing boats are berthed. Once the centre of the city's fishing industry, the neighbourhood today provides a unique blend of modern and traditional features.

Harbour Attractions: Learn about Iceland's maritime history by visiting the Maritime Museum. The display features everything from fishing gear to adventurers' stories. Don't pass up the opportunity to get a hands-on marine experience on board the iconic coast guard ship Óðinn.

Culinary Delights: With a variety of seafood eateries and cafes, The Old Harbour is a culinary haven. Savour daily fresh catch, Icelandic delicacies, and international fare while taking in the tranquil atmosphere of the harbour. Many places have seaside views from their outside chairs.

Whale Watching Tours: From the Old Harbour, set out on a whale-watching excursion. Many tour companies provide trips to see the local waters' magnificent whales, dolphins, and seabirds. It's a chance to get in touch with Iceland's amazing marine biodiversity.

Feel the artistic vibe as you stroll around the coastline of Old Harbour, which is adorned with vibrant sculptures and street art. Pause to admire the fusion of artistic expression and nautical heritage on display in these outdoor exhibits.

Harbour Hot Tubs: Take a swim in the geothermal hot springs along the harbour for a distinctly Icelandic experience. With a view of the mountains and sea, these outdoor hot tubs offer a tranquil bath that perfectly combines leisure and the great outdoors.

A lively atmosphere is created by the Old Harbour, which is a year-round centre of activity that hosts festivals and events. Events ranging from seafood festivals to cultural festivities are held periodically, bringing life to this ancient site.

Purchasing and mementos:

Browse the stores and boutiques lining Old Harbour. Find handcrafted items made nearby, mementos with a maritime theme, and distinctive Icelandic designs. It's a great chance to bring a little bit of Old Harbour home with you.

Walks Along the Harbour: Take leisurely strolls along the harbour, particularly while the stunning Icelandic sunsets are in effect. An atmosphere of peace and magic is created by the views of Mount Esja across the water and the color-changing sky.

To sum up, Old Harbour in Reykjavik is a diverse attraction that combines history, cuisine, art, and scenic beauty. The Old Harbour welcomes you with open arms, whether you're looking for a peaceful seaside experience or cultural insights.

Reykjavik Art Museum.

The Reykjavik Art Museum is a cultural landmark that provides an engrossing tour of Iceland's current art scene. Here's a guide to help make the most of your visit for those who are keen to tour its galleries and exhibitions.

Numerous Places:

There are three different venues for the Reykjavik Art Museum: Ásmundarsafn, Kjarvalsstaðir, and Hafnarhús. Every location offers a different viewpoint on Icelandic art, which includes both classical and modern items.

Modern and Contemporary Art: Hafnarhús is a modern and contemporary art gallery situated beside the Old Harbour. Take in shows that highlight a vibrant spectrum of artistic expressions by Icelandic and international artists. The building of the museum itself provides an interesting background for the artwork on exhibit.

Ode to Jóhannes Kjarval at Kjarvalsstaðir: Honoring the memory of the well-known Icelandic painter Jóhannes S. Kjarval, this location showcases an extensive collection of his paintings and honors his legacy. In order to provide visitors a better knowledge of Kjarval's influence on Icelandic art, the museum regularly organizes rotating exhibitions.

Ásmundarsafn - Sculpture and Architecture: Ásmundarsafn is a must-visit place for fans of sculpture and architectural art. Housed in a structure that the sculptor Ásmundur Sveinsson himself designed, this museum features his vast collection and emphasises the harmonious coexistence of art and architecture.

Rotating Exhibitions: Keep track of the museum's programme for a variety of artists and subjects included in rotating exhibitions. Offerings at the Reykjavik Art Museum range from conventional paintings to contemporary installations, all of which are interesting and new.

Workshops and Guided Tours: Take advantage of the museum's workshops or guided tours to make the most of your visit. A knowledgeable guide will enhance your comprehension of Icelandic art by offering insights into the artworks, artists, and the larger cultural background.

Cafés and Relaxation Areas: Indulge in a moment of respite while basking in the creative ambience of the museum's on-site cafés. These areas frequently provide beautiful vistas and offer a calm setting for reflection.

Museum Shop: Before you leave, browse the museum shop for literature, unique items, and souvenirs inspired by art. This is a fantastic chance to bring home a piece of Icelandic art.

Accessibility and Operating Hours: For details on operating hours and any special events, visit the museum's website. The museums frequently serve a wide range of patrons, including families and art enthusiasts, and the locations are conveniently located.

To sum up, the Reykjavik Art Museum presents a diverse array of Icelandic artistic expression and ingenuity. Art fans and inquisitive tourists alike can enjoy a vibrant and stimulating experience at this cultural institution, whether their interests lie in modern art, classical art, or sculpture masterpieces.

Reykjavik, Maritime Museum

The Reykjavik Maritime Museum offers an enthralling window into Iceland's maritime past for both tourists and enthusiasts. This is your handbook for exploring the displays and learning about the rich maritime history kept within.

The marine Museum is well positioned in the very backdrop that helped to develop Iceland's marine identity, right in the middle of Reykjavik's Old Harbour. The aroma of the sea and the sight of docked boats greet you as you get closer, setting the scene for an exciting maritime journey.

Take a trip down Iceland's nautical history in chronological order with Viking Voyages to Modern Shipping. From the Viking Age to the modern shipping industry, the museum explores the island nation's maritime history. Exhibits cover a wide range of topics, from the latest innovations in current ship technology to ancient seafaring gear.

Interactive Simulators and Displays: With the help of these tools, you may fully immerse yourself in the maritime experience. Experience life on a fishing trawler, get your hands dirty with navigational tools, and have a greater understanding of the difficulties faced by mariners traversing the North Atlantic.

Historical Vessels: Explore the museum's docked historical vessels. These remarkably pristine vessels offer a palpable link to Iceland's maritime history. A former coast guard ship, the Óðinn offers insights into nautical life by allowing guests to access its decks and staterooms.

fisherman's Stories: The museum shares the intimate narratives of Icelandic fisherman in addition to historical artefacts. Visitors get a moving grasp of the struggles and victories endured by those who have braved the North Atlantic in search of a living via multimedia presentations and oral accounts.

Children's Corner: The devoted children's corner will be appreciated by families with young adventurers. Little ones may have fun learning about maritime history with interactive games, instructive exhibits, and stimulating activities.

Temporary Exhibitions: For a glimpse into particular facets of maritime history, such as fisheries management or marine folklore, check the museum's programme. Every visit is made more interesting by these changing exhibits.

Guided Tours: To learn more about the museum's displays and the intriguing tales that surround the artefacts, think about taking a guided tour. Skilled tour leaders offer background information, turning your visit into a customised boat adventure.

Gift store and Café: Finish your seafaring journey by stopping by the museum's gift store, which offers books and gifts with a nautical theme. With its expansive views of the harbour, the on-site café offers a pleasant place to relax.

Useful Information: For more about special events, ticket costs, and opening hours, visit the museum's website. Anyone visiting the Old Harbour region will find the Reykjavik Maritime Museum to be an interesting and convenient stop.

In conclusion, the Reykjavik Maritime Museum is a living reminder of Iceland's continued ties to the sea, not just a repository of artefacts. Regardless matter your interest in the history of maritime exploration, the experiences of fisherman, or the mechanics of seafaring, this museum provides a thorough and engaging learning environment for all visitors.

Reykjavik's Perlan

Reykjavik's Perlan, a notable landmark, provides tourists with a singular fusion of natural marvels and cultural encounters. This is your manual for discovering the marvels contained beneath this recognisable glass dome.

Perlan, also known as "The Pearl" in Icelandic, is an impressive architectural wonder perched atop Öskjuhlíð hill. Its glass dome, which reflects the sky and surrounding landscape, conceals an exploratory universe.

360-degree views:

Climb up to the observation deck for an incredible 360-degree view of Reykjavik and the surrounding area. Admire the skyline, the far-off mountains, and the Atlantic Ocean's enormousness. The observation deck is the perfect spot from which to photograph Iceland's capital's splendour.

Natural Wonders of Iceland:

Enter Perlan's Wonders of Iceland exhibition to take your senses on a tour of the natural beauties of Iceland. Take in interactive exhibits that feature geysers, glaciers, and the Northern Lights. Iceland's glacial vistas are frighteningly realistically recreated in the indoor ice cave.

Planetarium: Discover space in the cutting-edge planetarium at Perlan. Entertaining presentations combine knowledge with amusement, taking viewers to the outer corners of the universe. For both astronomy buffs and inquisitive minds, it's an incredible experience.

Discover the captivating realm of the Northern Lights at Áróra, the Northern Lights Centre. The science and mythology underlying the Aurora Borealis are revealed in this multimedia centre located within Perlan, bringing the wonder of this natural phenomenon to life.

Þríhnúkagígur Volcano: Through a virtual reality experience, Perlan transports you to the heart of Iceland. Explore the lava chamber of this inactive volcano for a close-up look at Iceland's natural treasures.

Café & Restaurant: Savour delectable fare at Perlan's rotating restaurant. The panoramic views and menu, which draws inspiration from Icelandic delicacies, create a dining experience that accentuates the breathtaking scenery that surrounds you.

Skywalk: The Skywalk is an exhilarating experience for anyone looking for an adrenaline rush. This glass walkway, suspended from the dome, offers a bird's-eye perspective of the city below. For the daring and the inquisitive, it is an adventure.

Practical Information: For details about Perlan's opening times, entry costs, and any upcoming special events, visit their website. There are several ways to get to the museum, making it conveniently accessible.

In conclusion, Perlan represents a tasteful combination of natural beauty and cultural discovery. Take in the breathtaking views from Perlan's glass dome, discover Reykjavik from a different angle, or simply enjoy a unique eating experience. Perlan caters to a variety of interests.

Open Air Museum in Reykjavik

In a distinctive and immersive environment, the Arbaejarsafn Open Air Museum welcomes guests to travel back in time and explore Icelandic history. This is your guide to discovering the carefully conserved cultural treasures within this living museum.

Historical Village Setting: Arbaejarsafn, which is located outside of Reykjavik, is a recreation of a typical Icelandic village that features homes and everyday life from the mid-1900s to the 19th century. Take a stroll along quaint lanes lined with carefully moved and renovated old buildings.

Genuine Architecture: Take in awe of the museum's genuine buildings, each of which reflects a distinct era in Icelandic history. Icelandic settlements have evolved over time, as evidenced by the architecture, which ranges from turf huts to timber structures. A palpable window into everyday life is offered by the period-appropriate artifacts that adorn many of these structures.

Exciting Exhibitions: Take a look within the museum's structures to see displays that highlight the social, cultural, and economic facets of life in Iceland throughout history. The exhibits provide a thorough overview of the history of the neighborhood, including everything from home goods to traditional crafts.

Living History Days and Special activities: Living history days and special activities bring Arbaejarsafn to life. Costumed performers may play situations from everyday life for visitors, making for an engaging and dynamic experience. Traditional dances, music, and artisan demonstrations are frequently featured at these festivals.

Seasonal Variations: The allure of the museum changes as the seasons do. Vibrant gardens flourish and outdoor activities are abundant in the summer. Winter creates a calm ambience, and certain structures could exhibit special holiday rituals that let guests partake in Icelandic celebrations.

Café and souvenirs: In the historical setting of the museum, indulge in traditional Icelandic fare while taking a breather at the café. Books on Icelandic history and culture, handicrafts, and unique items are available at the on-site souvenir shop.

Educational Programmes: With guided tours and practical exercises, Albaejarsafn offers educational programmes for schools and organisations. These age-appropriate programmes promote a greater understanding of Iceland's cultural heritage.

Useful Information: Visit the museum's website to learn about its future events, entrance costs, and opening hours. The museum offers a handy way to explore Iceland's past and is easily accessible by automobile or public transit.

In conclusion, the Arbaejarsafn Open Air Museum immerses visitors in the everyday activities and cultural development of Icelandic towns, providing more than just a window into the past. Arbaejarsafn is a fascinating and instructive experience, regardless of your interest in architecture, cultural history, or just travelling back in time.

The Blue Lagoon, Iceland's Geothermal Oasis

Tucked away in Iceland's surreal scenery, the Blue Lagoon is a geothermal marvel and a peaceful retreat. This is your guide to enjoying the tranquil waters and stunning surroundings of this well-known location.

Marvelous Geothermal:

The Blue Lagoon is a unique geothermal spa on the Reykjanes Peninsula, fed by mineral-rich waters rising from underground hot springs. It is located amid a lava field. The presence of silica, algae, and minerals in the water gives the lagoon its characteristic milky-blue color.

Taking a Thermal Bath Experience

Take a plunge into the Blue Lagoon's warm, mineral-rich waters. In addition to being calming, geothermal heat is also thought to provide skin-rejuvenating benefits. Discover the numerous areas of the lagoon, each with a unique atmosphere and temperature.

Silica Mud Masks: The lagoon offers free silica mud masks that can improve your spa experience. Apply the rich in minerals mud to your face and body, allow it to dry, and then wash it off in the warm waters of the lagoon. Several guests embrace this restorative ritual.

Lagoon vistas and Facilities: Take in expansive vistas of the surrounding volcanic terrain while floating amid the steam rising from the lagoon. With features including steam rooms, saunas, and relaxation zones, the Blue Lagoon complex guarantees a comprehensive wellness experience.

In-water Massages: Schedule an in-water massage for a genuinely decadent experience. Combining the therapeutic effects of competent professionals with the benefits of geothermal therapy, knowledgeable therapists massage you as you float in the mineral-rich waters.

Savour Icelandic food while taking in the scenery at one of the Blue Lagoon's dining establishments. The food options, which range from light nibbles to elegant dinners, go well with the peaceful setting. For a truly immersive dining experience, think about reserving a table overlooking the lagoon.

Skin Care Bar: Making use of the lagoon's geothermal qualities, the Skin Care Bar at Blue Lagoon provides a selection of skincare items. Indulge in opulent skincare products that draw inspiration from the distinct characteristics of the waters of the Blue Lagoon.

It is suggested to make reservations in advance for your vacation to the Blue Lagoon because of its high demand. This makes sure you get the time window you want and makes the entrance procedure run more smoothly.

Visit the Blue Lagoon and surrounding attractions together: The Reykjanes Peninsula, with its striking scenery, lava fields, and bridge connecting two continents, is one of the closest attractions.

In summary, the Blue Lagoon is a tranquil haven amidst Iceland's natural marvels, not merely a geothermal bath. The Blue Lagoon offers a remarkable voyage into peace, whether you're looking for rest, skincare advantages, or a distinctive geothermal experience.

Golden Circle in Iceland.

Though the experience changes with the seasons, one can enjoy the Golden Circle year-round. The summer months of June through August bring long days, beautiful scenery, and brilliant hues. Winter, which lasts from December to February, offers the possibility to see the Northern Lights and a wintry, enchanted environment. There is a balance between both extremes in the spring and autumn.

Leading Attractions

Discover the historic location of Iceland's first parliament at Þingvellir National Park.

Dive or snorkel in the unusual underwater chasm known as the Silfra Fissure.

Witness the spouting geysers at the Geysir Geothermal Area, particularly the well-known Strokkur.

For information regarding geothermal activity, go to the Geysir Centre.

Gullfoss Waterfall: Admire the stunning two-tiered waterfall that plunges into the gorge.

For various vantage points and photo ops, stick along the trails.

Admire the impressive volcanic crater with a lake at its base, the Kerid Crater.

For sweeping views of the surroundings, stroll around the rim.

Top Travel Advice:

Drive or Take a Guided Tour: Getting to the Golden Circle by Car is a breeze. Having a car rental gives you flexibility.

Popular trips with skilled guides offering insights are guided tours.

Arrive Early or Late: Visit sights either early in the morning or later in the evening to avoid crowds.

This can offer a more tranquil experience, particularly at well-known locations.

Pack necessities:

When exploring, dress comfortably and put on solid shoes.

Bring snacks, water, a camera, and clothing appropriate for the weather.

Photographing Tip: Appreciate the beauty of nature and the shifting scenery.

To get the ideal photo of a geyser eruption in Geysir, be patient.

Planning Travel:

Travel Agents:

Golden Circle trips are provided by a number of trustworthy tour companies.

Look at options and select depending on your preferences, inclusions, and reviews.

Online Resources: You can reserve a lot of excursions online by using resources like GetYourGuide or Viator.

For popular tours, check costs, read reviews, and make reservations in advance.

Self-Drive: Take a rental automobile and go at your own speed around the Golden Circle.

Make sure your car is equipped for Icelandic driving conditions and plan your itinerary.

Combo excursions: Take into account combo excursions that incorporate visits to nearby farms or other sites, such as the Secret Lagoon.

These may offer a more thorough experience.

The Golden Circle, which offers a wide variety of historical landmarks and natural beauties, is a must-visit in Iceland. Exploring the Golden Circle is a journey into the heart of Iceland's rich past and magnificent scenery, whether you opt for a guided tour or a self-drive excursion.

Chapter 2

Visa and Entry Requirements

Visa-Free Admission

As a participant in the Schengen Area, Iceland permits visitors from numerous nations to enter the country for brief visits of up to 90 days during a 180-day period without a visa.

For a list of nations exempt from visa requirements, visit the official website of the Icelandic Directorate of Immigration.

2. Countries Needing a Visa:

You must apply for a Schengen visa through the Icelandic embassy or consulate in your home country if your nation is not exempt from requiring one.

To account for processing times, start the application procedure well in advance.

3. Applying for a Schengen Visa:

Fill out the application for a Schengen visa, which can be obtained in person or online at the embassy.

Get the necessary paperwork together: a letter of intent, a passport, passport-size pictures, a travel schedule, evidence of lodging, travel insurance, and proof of finances.

Make an appointment with the consulate or embassy of Iceland.

4. Interview and Appointment:

Show up for the appointed time and with the necessary paperwork.

Get ready for the consulate officer's interview. Give succinct, truthful responses about your intended route, reason for visiting, and ties to your native nation.

5. Processing Time for Visas:

It is best to apply well in advance of the day you plan to visit, as visa processing dates can vary.

If available, check the status of your application via the embassy's online portal.

6. Airport Arrival at Keflavik International:

Present your passport, visa, and any supporting documentation to Icelandic immigration officials upon arrival.

Make sure your passport is good for at least three months after the day you plan to go.

7. Licences to Reside:

You may require a residence permit if you intend to stay in Iceland for a period longer than ninety days.

Use the Icelandic Directorate of Immigration to submit an application for a residency permit.

8. Crucial Advice:

Requirements for visas can vary, so stay informed.

Examine the COVID-19 travel prohibitions and guidelines, since they can have an impact on your admission.

Consult the Icelandic consulate or embassy for information particular to your circumstances.

Following these recommendations can help you go through the visa and admission processes with ease, making your trip to Reykjavik, Iceland, easy and enjoyable. To ensure that you have the most recent and accurate information, always consult authoritative sources.

Things to pack on your travel preparation to Reykjavik, Iceland.

Warm Clothes: Bring layers, such as insulated clothes, a waterproof jacket, and thermal pants.

Given Iceland's erratic weather, having a high-quality, windproof, and waterproof jacket is essential.

Sturdy Footwear: For exploring a variety of terrain, comfortable, waterproof hiking boots or sturdy walking shoes are a must.

Decorative Items for Chilly Weather:

In particular during the winter, carry a warm hat, gloves, and a scarf to protect yourself from chilly winds.

Your feet will stay toasty while engaging in outdoor activities with thermal socks.

Swimsuit: Remember to pack your swimwear so you may have a dip in the well-known Blue Lagoon and other geothermal pools.

Daypack: When going on excursions, a compact, waterproof daypack comes in handy for holding necessities.

Bring an appropriate adaptor and voltage converter if necessary, as Iceland utilizes Type C/F electrical outlets, which are similar to those in Europe.

Reusable Water Bottle: Take advantage of the many clean water sources to fill up your reusable water bottle and stay hydrated.

With a camera and binoculars, you can take pictures of the breathtaking scenery and animals.

Binoculars are helpful for viewing distant objects and observing birds.

Power Bank: Make sure your electronics are fully charged, particularly if you're taking pictures or using navigation programmes.

Travel documentation: Make sure you have your passport, any essential travel insurance documentation, and a visa if needed.

Travel Adapters: Please carry the appropriate adapters for your gadgets as Iceland uses Europlug Type C/F electrical outlets.

Travel-sized Toiletries: Bring any specialized personal care products you need together with travel-sized toiletries like body wash, conditioner, and shampoo.

Medicines & First Aid Kit: Don't forget to pack a basic first aid kit and any prescription prescriptions you may require.

Reusable Shopping Bag: Since Iceland is environmentally sensitive, it can be helpful to have a reusable bag when making any purchases.

Travel Reference Books and Maps: Think about packing a reference book or maps for Reykjavik and the surrounding area.

Snacks: Bring some non-perishable food with you for outdoor activities so you can stay energized.

Invest in weatherproof equipment, such a waterproof phone case and a rain cover for your backpack.

A notebook and pen can be used to record crucial information when travelling or to keep a travel journal.

Portable Umbrella: In addition to being essential in wet weather, a little umbrella can also be helpful.

Adventurous Spirit: Lastly, to truly appreciate the singular experiences Iceland has to offer, bring an adventurous spirit and an open mind.

The weather and daylight hours in Iceland can vary greatly, so don't forget to adjust your packing list according to the particular season and the activities you have scheduled.

Chapter 3

To places To Visit.

~Hallgrimskirkja

Reykjavik's famous church, Hallgrimskirkja, commands attention from the cityscape thanks to its unusual architecture. Discover the following areas and inside this architectural wonder:

Wonder of Architecture:

Admire the church's striking architecture, which drew inspiration from Icelandic features like glaciers and basalt columns.

To see expansive views of Reykjavik and its surroundings, ride the lift to the summit.

Wander along the bustling street that leads from Hallgrimskirkja, Skólavörðustígur, which is dotted with cafes, boutiques, and stores.

Look around for shops that sell crafts, souvenirs, and designs with an Icelandic flair.

Visit the neighboring Einar Jónsson Sculpture Garden to view a selection of works created by Iceland's inaugural sculptor.

Reykjavik Roasters: Enjoy locally roasted coffee at this quaint café near Hallgrimskirkja.

Savor the laid-back ambiance and maybe a couple of pastries.

Sólfar (Sun Voyager) Sculpture: Make your way to the shore to take in the stunning sculpture of a Viking ship, Sólfar (Sun Voyager).

Take pictures of this famous site with the sea and mountains in the background.

Harpa Concert Hall: Take a stroll down the shoreline to this eye-catching glass building, which holds performances and cultural activities.

Examine the external architecture and see if there are any exhibitions or events taking place.

Old Harbour Area: If you have time, visit the neighboring Old Harbour area.

Visit the Reykjavik nautical Museum to learn about nautical history, or have dinner at one of the seafood eateries.

Tjörnin (The Pond): Take a stroll around this tranquil pond that is encircled by quaint buildings.

It's a serene haven in the middle of the city and a lovely place to observe birds.

Austurvöllur Square: Make your way to Austurvöllur Square, a major plaza encircled by antique shops and buildings.

It's a well-liked location for gatherings, particularly during festivals and events.

Parliament House: Constructed in 1881, the Parliament House (Alþingishúsið) is a historically significant edifice that is located nearby and serves as the seat of Iceland's parliament.

Explore the City Centre: Spend some time discovering Reykjavik's City Centre, which is home to colorful street art, a wide variety of restaurants, and important cultural sites.

The area around Hallgrimskirkja offers a lovely fusion of cultural discovery, architectural genius, and picturesque landscapes. This part of Reykjavik guarantees an unforgettable experience, regardless of your interests in history, art, or just taking in the ambiance.

Laugavegur: Reykjavik's Vibrant Shopping Street.

Laugavegur Shopping Delights: Local businesses: Discover distinctive clothing, jewelry, and design at these neighborhood Icelandic businesses.

Seek for products that highlight Iceland's creative flair and are designed by its designers.

Outdoor Gear Stores: Visit outdoor and adventure gear stores to prepare for your Icelandic travels.

Get top-notch gear for outdoor pursuits including hiking, camping, and exploring untamed areas.

Galleries: Visit the galleries strewn over Laugavegur to discover modern Icelandic art.

These galleries feature a variety of artwork, from sculptures to paintings, showcasing Reykjavik's creative scene.

Bakeries and Cafés: Stop by one of the quaint bakeries or cafés that line the street for a snack.

Take a look at some Icelandic delicacies, sip coffee, and take in the culture.

Booksellers: Check out Icelandic modern fiction, poetry, and sagas at your neighborhood bookshop.

You can discover hidden gems of Icelandic literature by exploring bookshops that provide English translations of their titles.

Vintage and Used Stores: Look through vintage and used stores to discover interesting items.

Discover apparel, accouterments, and unique pieces with a historical flair.

Design Shops: Visit specialized boutiques to immerse yourself in Icelandic design.

These shops feature clothes and home decor items that highlight the style and practicality of Icelandic design.

Record Stores: Music lovers interested in Icelandic and foreign vinyl can peruse record stores.

Explore a wide range of genres, including the sounds produced by regional musicians.

Souvenir Shops: Purchase mementos featuring Icelandic culture from a variety of shops.

Look for traditional Icelandic gifts, handmade crafts, and woolen products.

Admire the colorful paintings and street art that adorn the buildings along Laugavegur.

A large number of these pieces of art add to Reykjavik's vibrant and creative atmosphere.

Get Ready for Nightlife: As dusk draws near, check out stores that support Reykjavik's nightlife.

Buy chic apparel, accessories, or Icelandic spirits for a night on the town.

Food Markets: There are food markets in a few areas of Laugavegur.

Discover the local specialties, fresh products, and a taste of Icelandic cuisine by visiting these markets.

Practical Advice: You can stroll and browse the stores at your leisure because Lagunavegur is a pedestrian-friendly area.

Look out for street entertainers and cultural events that happen sporadically on the street.

To properly appreciate the range of shops and the street's artistic charm, visit during the day.

Laugavegur is a vibrant thoroughfare that perfectly captures the essence of Reykjavik's business, culture, and inventiveness. It is more than just a shopping street. Whether you're an avid shopper or just a tourist, a trip to Laugavegur provides a fun exploration of Icelandic flair and style.

Safnahúsið: The National Museum of Iceland.

Historical Journey: Safnahúsið, the National Museum, has fascinating displays that will engross you in Iceland's past.

Explore exhibits, documents, and artifacts that chart the cultural development of the nation.

Explore the permanent exhibitions that highlight the Age of Reformation, medieval history, and Iceland's settlement.

Learn about the nation's distinctive history, which includes manuscripts from the Middle Ages and sagas.

Temporary Exhibitions: Look for short-term shows that offer new insights into the history and culture of Iceland.

These revolving exhibits frequently explore particular subjects or eras.

Engage with interactive displays to add entertainment and information to your visit to the museum.

Multimedia presentations and touch-screen panels provide a contemporary method of storytelling.

Browse the vast collection of medieval manuscripts and documents housed in the Árni Magnússon Manuscript Collection.

This compilation offers an insight into Iceland's literary past.

Programmes for Education: Safnahsië provides workshops and guided tours as part of its educational offerings for schools and organizations.

These age-appropriate programmes provide an understanding of Icelandic history and culture.

Museum Shop: For one-of-a-kind books, gifts, and souvenirs influenced by Icelandic history and culture, stop by the museum shop.

Conference Centre and Concert Hall in Harpa:

Admire the architectural marvel that is Harpa, a magnificent concert hall and convention center.

The glass facade of the structure captures the play of light and reflects the landscapes of Iceland.

Concerts and Performances: See the schedule for upcoming events, concerts, and performances at Harpa.

The location presents a wide variety of cultural events, including modern and classical concerts.

Harpa Guided Tours: Take a guided tour of the building to discover more about its design, architecture, and cultural significance.

Investigate the different spaces, such as the Eldborg Concert Hall.

Eldborg Concert Hall: Known for its superb acoustics and contemporary design, try to see a show in the Eldborg Concert Hall.

International and Icelandic performers perform in the hall.

Harpa's Dining Establishments:
Savor a range of meals while taking in the scenery at Harper's restaurants and cafés.

The expansive view of the mountains and harbor from the eating area is magnificent.

Enjoy the shifting hues of Harpa's glass facade, particularly in the winter when the northern lights are visible.

The structure is transformed into a work of art for creative light shows, adding to Reykjavik's lively nightlife.

The Areas Around Harpa: Take a leisurely stroll around Harpa to take in the sights of the harbor and the surrounding outdoor artwork.

The surroundings offer a lovely backdrop for a day or night out.

Practical Advice: For information on upcoming shows, events, and performance dates, visit the websites of Harpa and Safnahúsië.

For a comprehensive understanding of Icelandic history and modern art, think of tying together a trip to the National Museum with a cultural event at Harpa.

Austurvöllur: Reykjavik's Central Square

Historical Significance: Surrounded by significant buildings, Austurvöllur is a historic square located in the center of Reykjavik.

It has served as a focal point for numerous events during Iceland's history.

The Parliament House, Alïingishúsið, is located on the square and has served as Iceland's legislative assembly's seat since 1881.

Admire this historic building's architecture and significance.

Cafés and Restaurants: You can have a meal or a cup of coffee in any of the quaint cafés and restaurants that surround Austurvöllur.

It's a terrific place to take in the vibe of the city and people watch.

Outdoor Seating: Many restaurants have outdoor seating during nice weather, letting you enjoy your meal or beverage outside.

Summertime brings a very lively atmosphere to Austurvöllur.

Protests and Gatherings: Throughout Iceland's history, the square has played host to a number of protests and gatherings.

Austurvöllur continues to be a significant platform for public discourse and involvement in the community.

Events and Festivals: Find out what events and festivals Austurvöllur could be hosting.

It's a hub for festivities, gatherings, and cultural events.

Aðalstraeti: Reykjavik's Historic Street

Oldest Street in Reykjavik: Dating back to the early days of the city's settlement, Aðalstræti is one of Reykjavik's oldest streets.

Take a stroll down this charming ancient street to soak in the atmosphere.

Explore the history of the city by paying a visit to the Reykjavik City Museum, which is situated on Aðalstræti.

See displays that illustrate Reykjavik's evolution from a sleepy hamlet to a cutting-edge metropolis.

Admire the architecture along Aðalstræti, where traditional and contemporary buildings coexist.

The historic character of the street has been retained in part by meticulous preservation of certain structures.

Explore the potential cultural and artistic spaces located along Aalestrachti.

The street is renowned for its unique assortment of artistic hubs and galleries.

Boutiques & Stores: Explore Aðalstræti's boutiques and stores for distinctive products, such as crafts and designs from Iceland.

It's a terrific spot to get gifts and souvenirs with a dash of regional flair.

Cafés and Bakeries: Take a leisurely stroll along Aðalstræti and stop at one of the cafés or bakeries.

The street is a nice place for a bite or coffee because of its laid-back atmosphere.

Possibilities for Walking Tours: Many walking tours of Reykjavik's historic attractions include a stop at Aðalstræti.

Tours led by guides shed light on the significance and history of the street.

Practical Advice: If you want to see the local scene and explore historical buildings, think about spending a day in Austurvöllur and Aðalstræti.

Both places are conveniently reachable on foot from the main center of Reykjavik.

Vibrant city life, cultural diversity, and historical significance are all combined in Austurvöllur and Aðalstræti. Discovering Reykjavik's political past or just meandering through quaint alleys are two compelling experiences you can have at these places.

Tjörnin: A Tranquil Oasis in Reykjavik

Calm Atmosphere: Tjörnin, a charming pond in the center of Reykjavik, provides a calm diversion from the hustle and bustle of the city.

Savor the peace by taking a leisurely stroll around the pond's edge.

Bird Watching: With a wide variety of waterfowl, such as swans, ducks, and geese, Tjörnin is a heaven for bird lovers.

Locals and tourists alike are drawn to the region to see and capture images of the varied birds.

Seasonal Variations: Take note of the seasonal variations in and around Tjörnin.

The pond might freeze in the winter and turn into a winter wonderland; in the summer, it will be full of colorful blooms and lush vegetation.

Reykjavik's City Hall (Ráðhús): Take in the building's architecture as you stand by Tjörnin.

The architecture of the building includes features that pay homage to Iceland's natural scenery.

Visit the Reykjavik City Library, which is situated close to Tjörnin.

The library is a popular venue for cultural activities, and the neighborhood is enhanced by its contemporary architecture.

Restaurants and Cafés: Unwind at one of the eateries or cafés that offers views of Tjörnin.

Savor a meal while taking in the picturesque surroundings and the ocean.

Discover the sculptures and art installations that encircle Tjörnin.

The region has elements that enhance the pond's and its surroundings' visual beauty.

Botanical Garden: For a tranquil getaway, head to the adjacent Reykjavik Botanical Garden.

Discover this verdant haven's varied plant life and themed gardens.

Views of Harpa Concert Hall: From the area of Tjörnin, stroll along the waterfront for expansive views of Harpa Concert Hall. The striking combination of contemporary building and natural surroundings makes for an enthralling spectacle.

Austurvöllur Square: Not far from Tjörnin, stroll to Austurvöllur Square.

The Parliament House and cafés encircle the square, which serves as a historic hub.

Shop till you drop at Laugavegur, Reykjavik's major retail avenue, which is just a short stroll from Tjörnin. Continue your journey there.

Explore the lively ambiance, boutiques, and cafés in this well-liked shopping center.

Practical Advice: Bring snacks or a light supper; Tjörnin is a great place for a leisurely stroll or picnic.

Come at various times of the day to take in the shifting atmosphere, which ranges from morning peace to nighttime contemplation.

Tjörnin and its environs provide a well-balanced experience of urban life, culture, and environment. For those who enjoy nature, bird watching, or just a quiet get-away, Tjörnin offers a quaint refuge right in the heart of Reykjavik.

Laugardalur Reykjavik

Visit Laugardalslaug, the largest geothermal swimming pool in Reykjavik, to immerse yourself in the local way of life.

Take a dip in the Olympic-sized pool, unwind in the hot tubs, and partake in the traditional Icelandic ritual of drinking geothermally heated water.

Laugardalsvöllur Stadium is worth visiting if you're a sports lover.

The Icelandic national football team plays its home games in the stadium, which also serves as the venue for other athletic events.

Grasagardur Park and the Botanical Garden: Take a tour of the Reykjavik Botanical Garden to see a wide variety of flora.

Grasagardur Park, which is next to the garden, offers a tranquil area for a stroll.

Laugardalur Park: Take a stroll through this verdant park that has walking trails and leisure spaces.

Locals love going to the park for sunny days, outdoor activities, and picnics.

Visit the Family Park and Zoo in Laugardalur if you are traveling with family (Fjolskyldu- og Husdyragardurinn).

Visit Icelandic farms and take part in family-friendly events at this informative and exciting location.

Laugardalsholl Arena: See what's happening at this multipurpose space that hosts exhibitions, sporting events, and concerts.

The arena's schedule might feature a variety of shows and entertainment events.

Explore the Reykjavik Park and Zoo, which is home to both domestic and native animals (Reykjavikur Botanisk Gardur).

You may learn about Icelandic farm animals and wildlife at the zoo.

Kjarvalsstadir - Reykjavik Art Museum: Proceed in the direction of Kjarvalsstadir, which is a section of the museum.

The renowned Icelandic artist Johannes S. Kjarval artwork is on display in this museum.

Facilities for Sports and Recreation: Laugardalur is a center for sports and recreation, with facilities for tennis, mini-golf, and athletics among other sports.

Laugardalur offers a wide range of activities, so it's perfect for anyone searching for something to do when they're not into athletics.

The Laugardalslaug Campground:

Laugardalslaug Camping Site is a handy spot if you enjoy camping.

Savour camping in the wilderness with convenient access to Reykjavik's facilities.

Practical Advice: Verify the hours of operation and any admission requirements for attractions like the Reykjavik Park and Zoo and Laugardalslaug.

For those without a car, Laugardalur is easily accessible by public transit.

A combination of outdoor activities, cultural encounters, and family-friendly attractions may be found by traveling eastward to Laugardalur. For guests of all ages, Laugardalur offers a wide variety of activities, including sporting events, botanical garden exploration, and relaxing in geothermal pools.

Perlan: Reykjavik's Iconic.

Panoramic Views: Known as "The Pearl" in Iceland, Perlan is a well-known monument featuring distinctive construction.

For amazing sweeping views of Reykjavik, the surrounding mountains, and the ocean, visit the observation deck.

Wonders of Iceland display: Go inside Perlan to explore the "Wonders of Iceland" display.

Through interactive exhibits, such as those featuring glaciers, volcanoes, and the Northern Lights, this immersive experience highlights the nation's natural treasures.

Perlan's Dome Restaurant: Savor a unique dining experience at this rotating eatery.

Savor a lunch while taking in the always shifting panorama of Reykjavik as the restaurant gradually rotates.

The Áróra planetarium show at Perlan offers a simulation of the Northern Lights phenomena. Come and enjoy this experience.

The presentation brings the splendor of the aurora borealis to life by fusing science and art.

Öskjuhlíð: Recreation and Nature Area

Hiking paths: There are hiking paths and open areas at the hillside nature reserve Öskjuhlíð, which is close to Perlan.

Enjoy the beautiful scenery and clean air by taking a leisurely stroll in the verdant surroundings.

Discover Rauðhólar, a collection of red volcanic craters in Öskjuhlíð.

The region's geological appeal is enhanced by the distinctive color of these craters, which were created by volcanic activity.

Discover the Peace Tower, located on the summit of Öskjuhlíð, at Friðarsúlan.

To mark the 200th anniversary of Iceland's national assembly, it was built in 1990.

Thermal Pools and a Geothermal Beach at Nauthólsvík

Reykjavik's Neuthólsvík is a geothermal beach that offers a distinctive coastal experience.

Take a dip in the sea that is heated by geothermal forces or unwind on the golden beaches.

Saunas and Hot Tubs: At Nauthólsvík, take advantage of saunas and hot tubs to improve your beachside relaxation.

The warm contrast between the cool ocean waters and the geothermal facilities is evident.

Changing Facilities: Guests may easily enjoy the beach and hot pools in Nauthólsvík thanks to its well-equipped changing facilities.

Practical Advice: To enjoy both daytime and evening vistas, think of visiting Perlan at different times of the day.

For exploring the trails at Öskjuhlíð, wear comfortable shoes.

Remember to pack a swimsuit, towel, and any other beach necessities when visiting Nauthólsvík.

Perlan, Öskjuhlíð, and Nauthólsvík together provide a variety of activities, from leisurely strolls by the sea to exploring the surrounding wilderness and taking in the expansive city vistas. These places offer a well-rounded overview of Reykjavik, whether you're interested in outdoor sports, galleries, or just relaxing by the seaside.

Seltjarnarnes: Coastal Tranquility near Reykjavik

Grótta Island Lighthouse: Start your journey at Grótta Island, which is prominently shown by the Grótta Island Lighthouse.

Take pleasure in a picturesque stroll to the lighthouse, particularly during low tide when you can traverse the causeway to reach the island.

Seaside Walks: Enjoy leisurely strolls along Seltjarnarnes' coastal trails.

Enjoy the peace and quiet as you stroll along the shoreline and take in the views of the surrounding landscape, the far-off mountains, and the sea.

Grótta Geothermal Foot Bath: Discover Grótta Island's unique outdoor swimming oasis, the Grótta Geothermal Foot Bath.

In the winter, take in the coastal ambience, unwind in the warm waters, and maybe even catch a glimpse of the Northern Lights.

Seltjarnarneskirkja Church: Take a look at this contemporary church with a unique layout.

In Seltjarnarnes, the church is distinctive as a historical and architectural site.

Bakkatjörn birding: Discover the birdwatching spots surrounding Bakkatjörn, a tiny lake in Seltjarnarnes.

Birdwatching is common at this spot, especially in the migratory seasons.

Discover the local recreation area Ásvellir, where both locals and tourists love engaging in outdoor sports.

It provides playgrounds, green areas, and sports facilities.

Sundlaug Seltjarnarness: Swimming Pool: Take a dip at the community pool at Sundlaug Seltjarnarness.

Take advantage of the sauna, hot springs, and swimming areas while taking in Seltjarnarnes' breathtaking scenery.

Local Restaurants and Cafés: Take a look at the Seltjarnarnes area's restaurants and cafés.

These places provide you the opportunity to enjoy Icelandic food in a warm setting.

Practical Advice: If you intend to trek to Grótta Island at low tide, make sure to check the tidal schedule.

If you intend to explore the seaside walks, make sure you pack appropriately for the weather and wear comfortable walking shoes.

The tranquil hideaway of Seltjarnarnes is conveniently located near Reykjavik. Seen as a peaceful retreat with a hint of Icelandic flair, Seltjarnarnes provides activities such as birdwatching, geothermal bathing, and coastline walks.

Greater Reykjavik: Expanding the Horizon.

Investigate the Reykjavik Metropolitan Area, which includes the city and the communities that surround it.

This vibrant area stretches outside the municipal limits and has a wide variety of attractions.

Visit Kópavogur, a city renowned for its thriving art scene, for art and culture.

Discover the museums, art galleries, and cultural activities that enhance Kópavogur's artistic environment.

Discover the harbor town of Hafnarfjörður, renowned for its rich history and tradition.

Take a stroll around the quaint old town, pay a visit to the Hafnarfjörður Museum, and discover the peculiar realm of hidden folk and elves.

Visit the Árbær Open Air Museum, an outdoor museum that features historical Icelandic architecture and lifestyle, to take a step back in time and experience traditional living.

Get a taste of bygone eras of the country living inside the city bounds.

Enjoy the natural splendor of Mosfellsbær, which is surrounded by mountains and lush scenery, for recreation and nature.

Discover the outdoor activities, hiking trails, and hot springs in this charming area.

Grafarvogur shopping: Visit Grafarvogur for entertainment and shopping.

There are eateries, retail centers, and leisure centers in the vicinity for both locals and tourists.

Vesturbær: Old West District: Discover Reykjavik's Old West District, Vesturbær.

Explore its quaint streets, which are dotted with stores, cafes, and old homes.

Öskjuhlíð's Perlan: An Urban Nature Retreat

Discover urban nature at Öskjuhlíð, which has lovely walking routes and Perlan.

Admire the expansive vistas of Reykjavik while strolling through the adjacent green areas.

Peninsula of Reykjanes: Geothermal Wonders:

Visit the Reykjanes Peninsula, which is a part of the larger Reykjavik area.

See geothermal marvels such as the continent-spanning bridge, geysers, and Blue Lagoon.

Outdoor Activities in Akranes: Take in the sights of the seaside and outdoor activities in Akranes.

The town provides opportunities for strolling along the coast, discovering lighthouses, and taking in the nautical ambience.

Transportation Hub: Make use of the effective transit system in Greater Reykjavik.

Numerous sites are conveniently accessible due to the region's excellent bus and road connectivity.

Practical Advice: For easy exploration of Greater Reykjavik, think about combining rental cars with public transport.

For a comprehensive experience, check the schedules of several municipalities' museums, attractions, and events.

Beyond the city center lies Greater Reykjavik, which offers a fusion of natural beauty, cultural diversity, and urban sophistication. This varied area offers a tapestry of Icelandic experiences, regardless of your interests in art, history, nature, or outdoor recreation.

Chapter 4

Transport Options in Reykjavik.

Public Bus System (Strætó): For reasonably priced and practical transit across Reykjavik, make use of the Strætó bus system.

The vast bus system links many suburbs, neighborhoods, and tourist destinations.

City Biking: Make use of the city's bike infrastructure to adopt a sustainable form of transportation.

Reykjavik is a bike-friendly city with designated bike lanes and programmes for renting and borrowing bikes.

Renting a car allows you to go around Reykjavik and its surroundings at your own speed.

A variety of cars, including 4x4s for travels exploring Iceland's untamed landscapes, are available from car rental providers.

Taxi Services: In Reykjavik, taxis are easily found and may be reserved via applications or by hailing one on the street.

Taxis are convenient, but their cost is comparatively higher than that of other forms of transportation.

Ride-Sharing Services: For on-demand transportation, make use of regional options or ride-sharing services like Uber.

These services provide convenience through smartphone apps as an alternative to conventional taxis.

Walking: Take a stroll through Reykjavik's tiny city center.

You may explore the city's environment by walking to a lot of its stores, restaurants, and attractions.

Select Airport Shuttle Services to ensure easy transportation between Keflavik International Airport and Reykjavik.

These shuttles offer a hassle-free connection because they run on a schedule.

Car-Sharing Services: If you need temporary access to a vehicle, think about car-sharing services.

Certain companies provide flexible use of shared cars that are stationed at different locations.

Tour Buses: Take an organized tour bus to see some of the most well-known sights in and around Reykjavik.

Frequently, pick-up and drop-off services are offered for these tours from strategic places.

Boat Tours: Take a boat tour from the harbour to see Reykjavik from the water.

These tours could include excursions to neighboring islands, animal viewing, or views of the city skyline.

Helicopter Tours: Take a helicopter tour to get an aerial perspective of Reykjavik and the surrounding area for a singular viewpoint.

For individuals who are looking for adventure in particular, these tours frequently offer an amazing experience.

Usable Advice:

Get a Reykjavik City Card to gain entry to multiple museums and sites as well as unlimited bus transit.

Examine the public bus schedule and routes, particularly if you intend to utilise them to get to certain destinations.

There are many different ways to get around Reykjavik, so guests can select the one that best suits their needs and schedule. Reykjavik's transport system makes exploration easy and fun, regardless of your preference for the freedom of a rental car, the ease of public transport, or the breathtaking views from a boat or helicopter.

Dining, Entertainment in Reykjavik.

Michelin-starred Dill Restaurant serves modern Icelandic cuisine.

Experience: Savor a refined eating encounter at Dill, a restaurant renowned for its creative use of regional ingredients and contemporary takes on Icelandic cuisine.

Icelandic fish and grill are the specialties of Grillmarkaðurinn (Grill Market).

Experience: Savor a meal that features flavors from Iceland in a chic atmosphere. The restaurant's distinctive ambiance is enhanced by its design, which incorporates lava and reclaimed wood.

Fiskmarkaðurinn (Fish Market): Fish prepared in an inventive way.

Experience: Savor the harmonious blend of Asian and Icelandic flavors. With its selection of locally produced products and the freshest seafood, the tasting menu offers a gourmet adventure.

Matur og Drykkur: Icelandic traditional cuisine.

Experience: Savor traditional recipes-inspired cuisine and a variety of regional beers and spirits as you immerse yourself in Icelandic heritage.

International and Icelandic cuisine are served in Perlan Restaurant.

Experience: Dine at Perlan's rotating restaurant while taking in the expansive vistas. Savor a varied meal with flavors from around the world and locally.

International grill cuisine is served at Kol Restaurant.

Experience: Take in Kol's vibrant ambiance while savouring its varied menu of grilled foods and inventive beverages. Both locals and visitors find it to be a popular option because of the chic surroundings.

Entertainment and Nightlife:

Kaffibarinn: A trendy and renowned atmosphere.

Experience: Visit the well-liked and relaxed Kaffibarinn bar to immerse yourself in Reykjavik's nightlife. It's well-known for its lively energy, live DJs, and diverse crowd.

Slippbarinn: Chic cocktail bar with an elegant ambiance.

Experience: Slippbarinn, a stylish bar with beautifully made cocktails, is situated in the historic Reykjavik Marina. It's a fantastic spot to begin or end the evening.

Pablo Discobar: Fun and nostalgic atmosphere.

Experience: Visit Pablo Discobar to take a trip back in time to the 1980s. This retro-themed pub is a favorite among people looking for a distinctive nightlife experience since it blends nostalgia with a vibrant dance floor.

Mini Bar: Ambience: Cozy bar serving artisan beers.

Experience: Visit Micro Bar to sample a variety of craft beers brewed in Iceland. For beer lovers, the cosy atmosphere and kind staff make it a refuge.

Den Danske Kro has a classic Danish pub atmosphere.

Experience: Take pleasure in Den Danske Kro's laid-back vibe. It's a laid-back place for a night out, offering a large assortment of drinks and live music.

Recipes to Taste:

Plokkfiskur: A hearty fish stew typically cooked with potatoes, onions, and cod or haddock.

Hangikjöt: Smoked lamb, usually eaten at Christmas, but always available in some places.

Popular Icelandic dairy product skyr has a distinct texture and is comparable to yogurt. frequently savored with honey and fruit.

Lambakaefa: A festive buffet that lets you try a variety of lamb dishes all at once.

Try a traditional Icelandic hot dog (Pylsur) topped with ketchup, sweet mustard, remoulade, crispy onions, and raw onions.

Modern culinary innovation combined with traditional Icelandic flavors can be found in Reykjavik's food scene. Combine your eating adventures with a trip to one of Reykjavik's bustling pubs or nightclubs for a comprehensive understanding of the city's nightlife.

Best site out bars in Reykjavik

Reykjavik boasts a thriving pub culture that serves a wide range of patrons' preferences. The following is a list of some of Reykjavik's well-known and respected bars:

Kaffibarinn: A well-known pub distinguished by its hip setting and frequent live DJ sets. Both residents and visitors think highly of it.

Reykjavik Marina is home to the chic cocktail bar Slippbarinn. It provides sophisticated surroundings and well-made cocktails.

Micro pub: A small, welcoming craft beer pub featuring a large assortment of beers from Iceland and other countries. You can get guidance from the competent staff regarding their services.

Pablo Discobar is an 80s-inspired vintage bar with a bustling dance floor. It's a great and interesting place to spend a night.

Den Danske Kro: A welcoming and laid-back typical Danish tavern. Savor a selection of beers and sometimes live music.

Húrra: Húrra is a well-liked live music venue that holds events and concerts. It's a lively place in the city because of the diverse décor and lively crowd.

Boston: A vibrant pub with a laid-back vibe, Boston is well-known for its large drink menu and American-inspired cuisine.

Mikkeller & Friends: Located in Reykjavik and a part of the well-known Mikkeller brewery, this bar provides a wide selection of craft beers in an elegant atmosphere.

Skúli Craft Bar: An ever-changing assortment of regional and foreign beers served in a craft beer setting. For those who enjoy beer, the relaxed environment makes it a terrific place.

B5: A multipurpose space that opens as a restaurant in the afternoon and closes as a bustling nightclub. It's well-known for its lively environment and eclectic crowd.

Bryggjan Brugghús: This tavern and brewery offers a selection of delectable food options in addition to its own line of craft brews.

Dillon Whisky Bar: Dillon is the place to go if you enjoy whisky. It's a whisky lover's paradise, with a large selection of whisky and a kind atmosphere.

Keep in mind that Reykjavik offers a wide variety of nightlife, so the ideal pub for you may depend on your tastes in music, ambiance, and beverages. It's wise to try out a few and identify which ones fit well with your personal style.

Chapter 5

Accommodation Options in Reykjavik, Iceland.

Hotels: Icelandair Hotel Reykjavik Natura: A modern hotel with modern amenities and an emphasis on sustainability in the city center.

the middleHotel Arnarhvoll: Conveniently situated in the heart of the city and close to the Harpa Concert Hall, this hotel offers expansive city views.

Homestays and Guesthouses:

Grettisborg Apartments: Cozy self-catering apartments in a peaceful neighborhood that are yet easily accessible by foot from Reykjavik's downtown.

Heida's Home: A family-run guesthouse in a quiet neighborhood with a warm atmosphere and attentive service.

Unique Places to Stay:

The 101 Hotel is a chic boutique hotel with opulent amenities and a modern design located in the centre of Reykjavik.

Kvosin Downtown Hotel: This boutique hotel, which blends modern and historical design elements, is situated near the parliament building.

Hostels: Downtown Reykjavik HI Hostel is a lively hostel in the heart of the city that's perfect for travelers on a tight budget or looking for a sociable setting.

Reykjavik's Bus Hostel is a hip hostel with an emphasis on sustainability that provides reasonably priced lodging with up-to-date amenities.

Vacation Rentals: Airbnb: For a more individualized experience, utilize Airbnb to browse a range of flats, homes, and distinctive stays that are hosted by locals.

Another website that offers houses and apartments for rent that may accommodate varying party sizes and tastes is VRBO.

Combination Car and Lodging: CamperVan Rentals: Take into consideration hiring a camper van, which combines lodging and transportation into one. For those who want to explore Iceland's natural treasures, this is the best option.

Hótel Höfn: Located southeast of Reykjavik, this hotel in Höfn provides a "Sleep and Drive" package that combines lodging with vehicle rental services for easy travel.

Practical Advice: Reserve lodging well in advance, particularly during the busiest travel times.

Think about how your lodging will affect the locations of the sites you intend to see.

Verify reviews and ratings across a range of sites to be sure the lodging suits your needs.

There are many different lodging alternatives in Reykjavik to suit a variety of tastes and budgets. In this dynamic city, you'll discover lodging alternatives that suit your needs, whether you're more of a fan of a guesthouse or vacation rental for its warmth and convenience or both.

Moderately Priced Hotels in Reykjavik

Remember that costs can change depending on the time of year, the platform used for booking, and availability. Prior to booking, it is advised to verify the most recent prices and reviews:

Icelandair Hotel Reykjavik Natura: A contemporary establishment with an emphasis on sustainability that provides cozy accommodations and conveniences. It offers a calm atmosphere and is near to the city center.

Fosshotel Lind: With its central position, Fosshotel Lind is an ideal starting point for experiencing Reykjavik. The hotel offers a range of room alternatives for comfortable lodging.

the middleHotel Arnarhvoll: CenterHotel Arnarhvoll offers modern accommodations and convenient access to Reykjavik's attractions. Its central location, close to Harpa Concert Hall, and its panoramic city views complete its appeal.

Hotel Klettur: With a focus on comfort and simplicity, this modern hotel is conveniently located near Reykjavik's downtown, just a short stroll away.

the middleHotel Klopp: Located in the centre of Reykjavik, this quaint hotel has a welcoming ambiance and is close to a number of well-known attractions and restaurants.

Storm Hotel: In Reykjavik, the Storm Hotel is a contemporary and reasonably priced choice.

Because of its handy location, walking about the city is a breeze.

Nestled in the heart of Reykjavik's historic district, Hotel Reykjavik Centrum offers a blend of contemporary conveniences and a historic environment. It is near eateries, retail establishments, and cultural landmarks.

Icelandair Hotel Reykjavik Marina: With a distinctive and lively ambiance, this hotel is located near the harbor. The hotel is well-known for its cozy rooms and nautical-themed decor.

By Keahotels, the Skuggi Hotel offers a modern style and a convenient location. It offers a cosy lodging with convenient access to Reykjavik's top sights.

Keahotels' Reykjavik Lights Hotel:

Reykjavik Lights Hotel offers a chic and laid-back ambiance, inspired by Iceland's natural beauty. Just a short drive gets you there from the city center.

It's important to keep an eye out for any promotions, discounts, or package deals that hotels may be offering because these can affect how affordable your stay will be overall. Furthermore, you may occasionally get better deals by making your reservation directly with the hotel or through reliable online travel agencies.

Chapter 6

Best time to Visit Reykjavik.

Depending on your interests and goals, there is no set optimal time to visit Reykjavik. The key things to keep in mind during various seasons are as follows:

Summer (June to August): Benefits include pleasant weather, plenty of daylight (June sees nearly constant daylight), lush green scenery, and the ideal season for outdoor activities like hiking.

Cons: There may be more tourists and more expensive lodging, particularly in July.

Autumn (September to October): Benefits include less tourists than in the summer and the possibility of seeing the Northern Lights as the nights get progressively darker.

Cons: As the days become shorter, several tours and attractions can have shortened hours.

Winter (November to February): Benefits include the possibility to engage in winter sports like skiing or snowmobiling, as well as stunning winter scenery and chances to observe the Northern Lights.

Cons: Fewer daylight hours, lower temperatures, and the possibility that certain trips or attractions will be weather-dependent.

Spring (March to May): Benefits include longer days, warmer weather than winter, and the opportunity to see whales as they migrate back.

Cons: Some activities might not be completely operational until later in spring, and the scenery might still be covered with snow.

The shoulder seasons, which are late May and early September, have the following advantages: they provide a nice mix of better weather, less crowds than the summer months, and the opportunity to see both autumn and spring scenery.

Cons: There may be restrictions on some activities and the weather is still unpredictable.

The ideal time to visit Reykjavik ultimately relies on your interests and the things you wish to see or do. Winter is the best time to see the Northern Lights, while summer is best for outdoor exploration in more comfortable weather. There can be a balance between good weather and less people during shoulder seasons. Make sure to verify the availability of particular activities, daylight hours, and weather during the time of your stay.

Children attraction and activities
Outdoors Activities

There are lots of kid-friendly outdoor activities and attractions in Reykjavik. Here are some suggestions for activities that can be done both inside and outside:

Children's Activities:

Discover the Reykjavik Family Park and Zoo (Fjölskyldu- og Húsdúragarðurinn), where kids can interact with farm animals, have fun on the playgrounds, and take part in family-friendly events.

Visit Perlan to take in the interactive exhibits about glaciers, volcanoes, and the Northern Lights as part of the "Wonders of Iceland" exhibition. There are expansive views of Reykjavik from the observation deck.

Visit the Reykjavik marine Museum (Víkin sjávarútvegsmiðstöð) to learn about Iceland's marine history. Children can investigate displays on life at sea, fishing, and nautical technologies.

Tjörnin Pond and Park: Wander around this charming pond in the heart of the city, Tjörnin. In the neighbouring parks, kids can play on the playgrounds and feed the ducks and swans.

Visit Hafnarhús, a section of the Reykjavik Art Museum, which frequently hosts kid-friendly art-related activities and family-friendly exhibitions.

Family Outdoor Activities:

Discover the Laugardalur Valley, which has a park with playgrounds, sports facilities, and a geothermal swimming pool (Laugardalslaug). You can have a lot of fun outside there.

Explore the Borgarlínan Sculpture Park, an outdoor art area featuring sculptures influenced by Icelandic mythology and culture. Children will love the creative atmosphere.

Discover the past at the Árbær Open Air Museum, where a historical hamlet is created with traditional Icelandic buildings. In a participatory and instructive environment, families may learn about the past.

Enjoy the Reykjavik Botanical Garden (Reykjavíkurborg), where kids can learn about different plant species, stroll through themed gardens, and have fun in the open areas.

Hiking Trails: Look for family-friendly hiking trails in the area. Trails around Mount Esja are a popular choice since they provide beautiful views of Reykjavik and the surrounding area.

Visit Nauthólsvík Geothermal Beach for an unforgettable beach experience. Even in colder months, kids may enjoy a beach day because to the sea's geothermally heated surface.

While in Reykjavik, keep an eye out for family-friendly events and activities at the individual attractions, since many provide unique programmes to accommodate families and children.

Chapter 7

14 days itinerary in Reykjavik, Iceland

A 14-day plan that offers a combination of city experiences, natural wonders, and cultural discovery is provided for exploring Reykjavik and the surrounding areas:

Days 1-3: Touring Reykjavik

Day 1: City and Arrival First Off

When you get to Reykjavik, settle in at your lodging.

Explore the city center in the afternoon, taking in sights including Laugavegur retail district, Harpa Concert Hall, and Hallgrímskirkja.

leisurely evening spent at a nearby restaurant.

Day 2: Parks and Museums

See the Reykjavik Art Museum and the National Museum of Iceland.

Investigate the parks surrounding Tjörnin Pond.

Optional: Unwind at the geothermal Laugardalslaug pool.

Day 3: Öskjuhlíð and Perlan

Take in the expansive vistas when you visit Perlan.

Discover the Peace Tower and hiking routes on Öskjuhlíð Hill.

A leisurely evening in Reykjavik's centre.

Day 4–7: South Coast and the Golden Circle

Day Four: Circle of Gold

Go on a day trip to the Golden Circle, which includes stops at Gullfoss Waterfall, Geysir Geothermal Area, and Þingvellir National Park.

Optional: Have lunch at the Friðheimar greenhouse.

Day 5: Black Sand Beach and Waterfalls on the South Coast

Go to the coast in the south. See the waterfalls at Skógafoss and Seljalandsfoss.

Discover Reynisfjara's beaches with black sand.

Spend the night nearby.

Day 6: National Park Vatnajökull

Travel by car to National Park Vatnajökull.

Discover the Skaftafell region; there are hiking routes here for every ability level.

See Diamond Beach and Jökulsárlón Glacier Lagoon.

Day 7: Returning to Reykjavik and the Fjaðrárgljúfur Canyon

Take a beautiful hike at Fjaðrárgljúfur Canyon.

Later in the evening, return to Reykjavik.

Day 8–10: The Peninsula of Snaefellsnes

Travelling to Snæfellsnes on Day 8

Go via car to the Snæfellsnes Peninsula.

Stykkishólmur, a coastal village, is worth exploring.

See some of the nearby landmarks, such as Kirkjufell Mountain.

Day 9: National Park Snæfellsjökull

Explore the National Park of Snæfellsjökull.

Walk around the glacier Snæfellsjökull.

See the beach at Djúpalónssandur.

Day 10: Neighbourhood Towns and Go back to Reykjavik.

Visit the quaint seaside towns of Hellnar and Arnarstapi.

Later in the evening, return to Reykjavik.

Day 11–14: Travel to North Iceland and Leave

Day 11: Myvatn and Akureyri

Travel by car or plane to Akureyri, North Iceland.

Explore the Botanical Garden and Akureyri.

Go via the Lake Myvatn area by car.

Day 12: The Environment and Lake Myvatn

Discover Hverir and Grjótagjá, two of Lake Myvatn's geothermal wonders.

Take in the lava formations at Dimmuborgir and unwind in the Myvatn Nature Baths.

Day 13: Husavik and Dettifoss

See Europe's most potent waterfall, Dettifoss.

Take a car trip to Husavik to go whale viewing.

Go back to Akureyri to spend the night.

Day 14: Leaving

Depending on when you're leaving, continue your exploration of Akureyri or unwind before going to the airport.

Take off from Akureyri or return to Reykjavik in time for your international journey.

Don't forget to modify the schedule according to the weather, your preferences, and the particular attractions or activities you wish to prioritize. The varied and dynamic landscapes of Iceland offer a singular experience on each visit.

Essential Tips and Information for Travelers Visiting Reykjavik, Iceland.

Weather and Clothes: The weather in Iceland varies a lot. Include windproof and waterproof clothes in your layering. It's imperative to have insulated layers, a strong waterproof jacket, and quality hiking boots.

Temperatures can change even in the summer, so pack a variety of warm and airy outfits.

Money: The Icelandic Króna (ISK) is the unit of money in Iceland. Although credit cards are generally accepted, it's a good idea to have cash on hand for smaller businesses or locations outside of Reykjavik.

Language: Although English is commonly spoken, Icelandic is the official language. The majority of menus, signage, and information are in English.

Safety: Although Iceland is famed for its safety, proceed with caution. The weather can be difficult, particularly in the winter. Observe local guidance and keep yourself updated on road conditions.

Mode of transportation: Hiring a car is a great method to see Iceland's scenery. Make sure your rental car is appropriate for Icelandic driving conditions, particularly if you intend to venture off the main routes.
For city travel, Reykjavik also boasts a dependable public bus system (Straetó).

Power Outlets: The Europlug (Type C/F) power outlets are used in Iceland. If the plug type on your gadgets is different, bring adapters.

Wi-Fi and Connectivity: Major towns including Reykjavik have extensive Wi-Fi coverage. A local SIM card might provide you access to mobile data if you intend to travel to more isolated locations.

Natural Wonders: Honor the environment and adhere to the Leave No Trace philosophy. Avoid disturbing wildlife, stick to designated routes, and use caution while near cliffs and geothermal sites.
Look out for any limitations or closures, particularly in the spring when birds are breeding.

Northern Lights: Visit during the clear, dark months of September through April if you intend to hunt the Northern Lights. For best viewing, check aurora forecasts and avoid bright city lights.

Tap Water: Icelandic tap water is excellent and safe to consume. To stay hydrated, bring a reusable water bottle.

Opening Hours: Reykjavik operates on regular business hours; however, several smaller towns might only offer limited services, particularly on the weekends. Make appropriate plans and confirm the hours of operation for restaurants and activities.

Time Zone: During daylight saving time, Iceland is on Greenwich Mean Time (GMT) or Greenwich Mean Time +1 (GMT+1).

Health and Emergency Services: - Although healthcare can be expensive, medical services are first-rate. Make sure your travel insurance includes medical coverage. In Iceland, the emergency number is 112.

Local Etiquette: The people of Iceland are amiable and hospitable. Say "Góðan daginn" (Good day) to people and observe local traditions, such as removing your shoes when you enter a home. **15. Sun and Daylight: During the summer, Iceland has nearly constant daylight, also referred to as the Midnight Sun. Winter days, on the other hand, are brief and have little daylight. Be ready for shifting light levels.

Cuisine: Savour lamb, salmon, skyr (a dairy product similar to yogurt), and the well-known hot dog (pylsur), among other traditional Icelandic fare.
Remember that eating out can be costly.

Planning Tours & Excursions: - Reserve popular tours, such as the Blue Lagoon or Glacier treks, in advance to assure your seat. - Think about setting aside money for groceries or less expensive options. Tour timetables may be impacted by weather, so be mindful of cancellation rules.

Honour Local Wildlife: Iceland boasts a wide variety of birdlife. Observe these rules when visiting bird cliffs to prevent upsetting breeding birds. **19. Sun Protection: - The sun can be very strong even in lower temperatures. Bring a hat, sunglasses, and sunscreen.

Savor the Midnight Sun: - Make the most of the Midnight Sun if you're traveling in the summer. For a memorable experience, explore Reykjavik at midnight or go hiking in the wilderness.

Recall that the unspoiled scenery and lively culture of Iceland are what make it so beautiful. Cherish the unique experience you have in Reykjavik and beyond, appreciate the environment, and embrace the Icelandic way of life.

Chapter 8

Reykjavik Cultural Experience.

Iceland's capital city of Reykjavik presents a diverse cultural fabric that embodies the country's legacy and creative ethos. The main components of Reykjavik's cultural experience are as follows:

Art community: With lots of galleries and street art, Reykjavik boasts a thriving art community. See both traditional and contemporary Icelandic art at places like the Harpa Concert Hall and the Reykjavik Art Museum.

Music and Festivals: Reykjavik is the centre of Iceland's booming music scene. The city attracts both domestic and foreign musicians with its music events, which include Iceland Airwaves and Reykjavik Arts Festival.

Iceland is known for its rich literary heritage, and Reykjavik is home to state-of-the-art institutions such as the Reykjavik City Library. The city's literary life is enhanced by poetry festivals, book readings, and literary activities.

Architecture: Reykjavik's buildings combine modern and traditional Icelandic design elements. The innovative Harpa Concert Hall and the Hallgrímskirkja church are noteworthy landmarks.

Culinary Delights: Fresh, local products are prioritized in Reykjavik's diversified culinary scene. Discover Icelandic food in the city's restaurants, ranging from inventive creations to traditional lamb dishes.

Nightlife: There are a lot of bars, pubs, and clubs in Reykjavik, making for a vibrant nightlife. Take in the distinctive ambience at locations like Kaffibarinn or liven up small gatherings with music.

Language and Literature: An essential component of Iceland's identity is its native language. Explore Icelandic literature to learn more about the cultural narrative. This includes both modern and saga writing.

Local Events: Take part in events held locally to honor Icelandic culture. Events that showcase traditional crafts, folk music festivals, and cultural fairs are a few examples of these.

Major Events in Reykjavik:

Iceland. A well-known music festival called Airwaves features a wide variety of Icelandic and foreign performers. It's a celebration of the nation's music culture, taking place in a number of Reykjavik venues.

The Reykjavik Arts Festival is a multi-disciplinary arts celebration that offers events, exhibitions, and performances. It celebrates creativity and innovation by bringing together artists from around the world.

Every year, Culture Night (Menningarnótt) brings Reykjavik to life with a variety of cultural events, performances, and celebrations. Both residents and visitors honor the city's cultural richness on this day.

The Reykjavik International Film Festival (RIFF) is a gathering place for moviegoers and directors. RIFF presents a wide range of international film releases.

Independence Day (National Holiday): June 17th is Independence Day, which commemorates the establishment of the Republic of Iceland. Parades, concerts, and other cultural events are all part of the celebrations.

Reykjavik Pride is an all-inclusive celebration of diversity and LGBTQ+ rights. Reykjavik Pride includes a vibrant procession, musical performances, and activities aimed at fostering acceptance and equality.

Winter Lights Festival: An annual winter festival with light displays, musical performances, and cultural events that brighten Reykjavik. It gives the city a magical touch in the gloomy winter months.

Experiencing these festivals and Reykjavik's cultural attractions will help you gain a better knowledge of Iceland's history and vibrant, innovative culture. The city is a cultural center and the world's northernmost capital because of its dedication to the arts, literature, and music.

Chapter 9

Souvenir Shopping in Reykjavik, Iceland.

For those looking to buy souvenirs, Reykjavik provides a distinctive shopping experience with its modern design and blend of Icelandic customs. Here's a list of recommended products and fantastic stores for an unforgettable shopping trip:

1. Icelandic Woolens: Where to Shop: Boutiques such as Geysir and Álafoss are scattered around Laugavegur, the main shopping route. The Handknitting Association of Iceland also sells genuine handcrafted woolens.

Recommended Products: Lopapeysa, traditional wool jumpers from Iceland with elaborate patterns.

Wool blankets and socks are warm and exquisitely made.

2. Icelandic Design: Where to Buy: Visit design shops that feature the works of Icelandic designers, such as Epal, Kirsuberjatréð, and Kraum.

Suggested Items: Jewelry: Handmade pieces with inspiration drawn from Icelandic heritage and environment.

Icelandic design sensibilities are reflected in both traditional and modern home décor items.

3. Artifacts Inspired by Vikings: Hafnarfjörður's Viking Village or Reykjavik's specialty stores, such as The Nordic Store, are good places to shop.

Suggestions: Pendants depicting Thor's Hammer (Mjölnir), a representation of the power and defense of the Vikings.

Drinking Horns: Handcrafted with a genuine Viking feel.

4. Icelandic Skincare & Beauty: Shoppers can visit the city's pharmacies and Blue Lagoon-like establishments on Skólavörðustígur street.

Recommended Products: Blue Lagoon Skincare Line: Known for its nourishing qualities.

Products Made of Birch and Moss: Representing the pure nature of Iceland.

5. Handmade pottery: Where to Buy: You can find Icelandic pottery in a number of retailers, including Ástíór Helgason and Kirsuberjatréð.

Recommended Products: Icelandic-inspired plates and mugs with designs.

Handmade sculptures created by regional artists.

6. Icelandic Books and Literature: Where to Shop: Check out the gift shop of the Icelandic Phallological Museum or bookstores such as Eymundsson.

Recommended Reading: Icelandic Sagas: Classic books that depict the history of the country.

Explore modern Icelandic storytelling with these contemporary Icelandic novels.

7. Products Made from Reindeer and Fish: Where to Buy: specialized food stores and markets like Kolaportië Flea Market.

Suggested Products: Smoked Salmon or Arctic Char, delicacies from Iceland's seas.

Sausages or reindeer jerky are interesting and tasty snacks.

8. Icelandic Chocolate and Licorice: Where to Buy: There are many chocolate stores in Reykjavik, including Te & Kaffi for licorice and Omnom for chocolate.

Omnom Chocolate Bars are a handcrafted product made using ingredients from Iceland.

Lakkrís (Licorice): Comes in a variety of flavors and is a local favorite.

9. Handmade Glassware and Pottery: Where to Buy: Check out shops like the Icelandic Handicrafts Association and Mál og Menning.

The following products are suggested: Handmade bowls and plates that showcase Icelandic design.

Glass Art: Masterfully crafted by nearby glassblowers.

10. Icelandic Music: Recommended Items: To experience Icelandic music, check out record shops such as Smekkleysa and 12 Tónar.

Records on vinyl: Including a wide variety of Icelandic musicians.

Local Music CDs: Discover Icelandic musicians' distinctive sounds.

Recall:

Haggling over Prices: Icelandic stores do not typically engage in negotiations. Usually, prices are fixed.

Tax-Free Shopping: Travelers who make purchases over a specific amount are eligible to claim VAT. Observe the Tax-Free Shopping emblem.

The retail environment in Reykjavik offers a glimpse into the artistry and craftsmanship of Iceland. Whether you're drawn to contemporary art, traditional woolens, or regional specialties, the city's varied options guarantee that you'll take a little piece of Iceland's distinct charm home with you.